NAPLES
and POMPEII

by

DOMENICO REA
and CARLO GIORDANO

Translated by

PAUL GARVIN

BONECHI EDITORE
50122 FIRENZE - Via dei Rustici, 5

NAPLES

di DOMENICO REA

The great travellers of the past never failed to include Naples in their journey. They were attracted to it by the certainty of finding a world and a sort of people quite out of the ordinary. Even today, in a Europe subjected to the levelling action of progress, Naples still remains unique, a kind of country within a country, with its own particular customs and uses different from the rest of Italy, all the more striking and exciting from the contrast with the attempts at modernisation which, for reasons too complicated to explain, are unsuccessful in adapting themselves to the environment as they mostly do elsewhere. Naples owes this continuation of its instinctive vitality to the extrovert character of its inhabitants who can be said without exaggeration to belong to a peculiar class of the human species which can be labelled as "Neapolitan Man". A member of this species, who outside Naples displays a great capacity of adaptation to new surroundings and concealment

The **Molo Angioino,** the dockside with its spectacular passenger station for travellers to all parts of the world. At night the huge harbour takes on all the charm of unreality from the myriad lights of the liners at berth. By day the incomparable beauty of Vesuvius dominates the background.

One of the famous views of Naples with **Vesuvius, Castel dell'Ovo** and Via Caracciolo between the Town Hall and the sea. The harmonious lines of the landscape and the gulf lose nothing of their attraction from the picture-postcard effect of the scene. The continuous line of semicircles along the coast form a series of delightful bays and inlets.

of his origin, in his native city behaves in public as if he were in the privacy of his home with an enormous expenditure of energy in the performance of magnificent gestures which often seem to have no meaning beyond the pleasure he himself may derive from them. In this sense Pulcinella, the famous stock character of popular comedy (our Punch), is a typical Neapolitan. He can never achieve really comic or really dramatic effects but always remains within the limits of the grotesque or the farcical with his quips and jests and the wild exaggerated behaviour that marks him as a puppet, so much so that even when he is the victim of injustice and should claim our sympathy, his sufferings only make him ridiculous and an object of derision. His self-inflicted wounds are in reality a form of self-protection for saving his dignity and self-respect. If it were not so, it would be impossible to explain how it is that a people so inclined to misuse the talents nature has endowed them with should have produced Thomas Aquinas, Giovanni Battista Vico and Benedetto Croce, the three greatest Italian philosophers, and the heroic martyrs in the struggle for independence and the unification of Italy. Usually forbearing and easily contented, the Neapolitan is capable of sudden outbursts of revolt. Sensual and carnally-minded,

he can yet compose the tenderest love songs in honour of the spirit of woman. With his imagination full of the most exquisite foods, he prefers to eat simple dishes composed of flour, water and salt like spaghetti and pizza, made prodigious by the art with which they are flavoured by tomato and basil. This contradiction is present everywhere in Naples. Built on the sea, it turns its back to it and looks inland. Where light and sunshine should abound, there are dark alleyways and subterranean dwellings. Religious to a point verging on idolatry, the inhabitants can yet behave without any regard for moral scruples. And all this can be intimately felt and observed because life flows along unhampered even around the great city buildings. In Forcella, La Duchesca or Spaccanapoli you will find the same atmosphere, the same lights and colours, smells and odours, the same busy trafficking as to be found in any market or bazaar along the farthest shores of the Mediterranean. Invention and novelty are the order of 'the day. Only in Naples is it possible for a tourist to light upon something new which he himself has discovered — an object, a gesture, a word — and has escaped the notice of others and is not to be found in any guide book or traveller's account.

A view of the little port of **Mergellina** with a group of fishermen mending their nets. However picturesque the scene, life for the townsfolk generally means hard work.

Another view of the harbour at Mergellina. From spring to late summer it is always crowded with yachts and vessels of every shape and size, fishing boats and the romantic-looking pleasure boats for popular use. A large number of stalls and booths along the waterfront sell live fish, and oysters, clams and mussels and other shellfish served on plates and wrapped around with seaweed leaves with slices of lemon.

A night view of Naples seafront. Via Caracciolo is outlined by the row of dim lights at the base of the semicircle to allow the passer-by to see clearly every detail of the coast at Sorrento and the profile of Capri on the edge of the horizon.

Porta Capuana - Designed by Giuliano da Majano and erected in 1484, this is one of the best preserved and perhaps one of the most beautiful of the old gates dating from Renaissance times. The two towers are called by the names of Honour and Virtue. Nearby is the district of La Duchesca where you can find and buy practically anything. The over-excited atmosphere of the place tends to confirm the old saying that Naples is a devils' paradise.

Castel dell'Ovo - The unusual name (" Egg Castle ") is said to come from a legend going back to the time of the Roman poet Virgil, or maybe it only refers to the egg-shaped construction of the building. The castle was a central point in the turbulent history of Naples and in its underground dungeons many notable persons were imprisoned before being executed. In recent years its walls and towers are set alight during the Piedigrotta festival as part of the celebrations.

Borgo Marinaro - a place to visit and enjoy to the full without the fear of being taken for an inveterate sightseer. Naples here provides a synthesis of its much abused colourfulness, continually redeemed by a sense of discovery. Its harbour is filled with the small boats that figure so prominently in the old melodious Neapolitan songs with their combined themes of love and sea-fishing. Facing the sea a number of **trattorie** (small restaurants) offer abundant supplies of spaghetti and

pizza. Prominent among the jostling crowd under the arcade are the last examples of a dying race, the **scugnizzi,** boys who are ready to dive underwater like pearl-fishers to retrieve a coin you throw in. Visitors from every land converge here as if to fulfil a vow.

Piazza Municipio. This great square is the centre of the business life of the city with its banks, agencies and offices of all kinds, the Town Hall, the National Library and headquarters of big companies. The whole length of the square was once covered with holm-oaks which enabled pedestrians to cross from one end to the other without the risk of sunstroke, but unfortunately they were felled to allow for the traffic. The square adjoins the port where the liners at berth seem to be as tall as the buildings on land, the Castel Nuovo (or Maschio Angioino), and the delicate, austere setting of the Royal Palace gardens. The equestrian statue in the middle is of Victor Emmanuel II.

Castel Nuovo, the New Castle, so called to distinguish it from those already existing when it was built in the thirteenth century by Charles I of Anjou. Remodelled for comfortable living in the fifteenth century, it was for long the focal point of the bitter rivalries between the various royal families in the struggle for the throne. Famous people who stayed there include Celestine V, the 13th century pope who renounced the papacy, and Petrarch when on his way to Rome to be crowned poet laureate in the Capitol. Boccaccio has left us a good description of the worldly frivolous life that rotated around the Angevin court. Castel Nuovo tells us what a Renaissance castle was like: outside like a fortress, inside full of art and splendour. Today the huge building houses a library (Biblioteca di Storia Patria) containing thousands of books and rare manuscripts and records.

Piazza Plebiscito and **Church of San Francesco di Paola.** The square is like a fitting entrance hall to the Royal Palace which, with your back to the church, you can admire in its full extent. Once the happy hunting ground of flocks of pigeons, time has reduced the square to an unsightly parking place for cars. It contains the Prefecture and Palazzo Salerno. The two equestrian statues are of Charles III of Bourbon and Ferdinand I. The two horses and the figure of Charles are the work of Canova, while Ferdinand is by Antonio Calì.

The **Royal Palace** is remembered above all for the rather theatrical-looking) row of kings occupying niches (eight of them). Their origin is rather curious, due to an error of calculation on the part of the designer, Domenico Fontana. After a time cracks began to appear, and to repair the damage half the portico was filled in with this row of niches which, however, remained empty till 1888 when it was decided to put in the statues. They are (from left to right) Roger the Norman, Frederick II of Swabia, Charles I of Anjou, Alfonso of Aragon, Charles V, Charles II of Bourbon, Joaquin Murat, and Victor Emmanuel II. Inside the palace among other curiosities (various style furniture, carpets, chinaware etc.) are to be seen Ferdinand IV's study, the chapel used by Maria Cristina of Savoy, the throne of the Bourbons, and the famous silk hangings produced by the royal manufactory at San Leucio.

Royal Palace. The Great Staircase.

San Biagio dei Librai. This is just one section of the intermin-
able **Spaccanapoli,** a street narrow as a lane but straight as
a die that runs through the old town and cuts it in two. You
can visit the palaces and museums of Naples to improve your
mind, but it would be well to devote days and weeks to the
study of a street like San Biagio dei Librai and the adjacent
ones, for the pleasure of observing the incessant stream of life
that flows along them. Here one can conjure up in the imagination a vision of a world of the past and realise that
though from the material point of view it may have been
rather an uncomfortable one, at least that world was not
lacking in human warmth.

A barrow-man, the orig-
inal type of antique
dealer in Naples. He
would sell you anything
at a reasonable price
from a piece of Capo-
dimonte porcelain or a
Louis XV easy chair
to a fan painted by
Watteau.

Night view of the fountain in **Piazza Sannazzaro** which shows a siren with sea-horses and fish. The sea is a few yards away at Mergellina. The tombs of Virgil and the great Italian poet Leopardi are only a few yards away, up towards Fuorigrotta.

A small shrine, one of the thousands dotted along the walls of the streets in the poor quarters of Naples. These shrines were put up as an expression of popular devotion but they also served as a means of street lighting. The few street lamps that existed were continually being broken by thieves who prowled by night, and the famous Padre Rocco — whose life history would take too long to relate — had the bright idea of putting lamps in the shrines as a sign of devotion, thus solving the lighting problem as no one, naturally, would dare to touch them.

Galleria Umberto I, facing San Carlo theatre, built 1887-90 and planned by the architect Emanuele Rocco. It is octagonal in form and topped by a glass and iron dome. It can be considered in a way as the heart of the city, not only because it stands at the meeting point of streets and a square famous in history and bustling with life, but also because in past decades it was the theatrical centre of Naples. Today it is a meeting place for writers of Neapolitan songs.

Obelisk erected in the middle of **Piazza San Domenico Maggiore** as a votive offering after the terrible plague of 1656. On the top is a bronze statue of St. Dominic.

16

Church of the Gesù Nuovo in **Piazza del Gesù (Piazza della Trinità Maggiore).** After Santa Chiara and San Domenico Maggiore this church is the most popular in Naples. Its beehive façade is not easily forgotten, especially if taken in conjunction with the amusing thirty-metre-high **Spire of the Immacolata,** a characteristic expression of Neapolitan baroque. The church contains frescoes by Solimena, Massimo Stanzione, Luca Giordano and other famous artists.

Church of **San Giovanni in Porta,** also called " *Gesù delle Monache* ". The façade gives a good idea of Neapolitan religious sentiment, genuine and profound but with an instinct for the theatrical that it always seeking an outlet. Faith is a kind of scenic representation of life, as in the Neapolitan Christmas crib.

CAPODIMONTE

Capodimonte Palace, originally a hunting lodge of Charles III, today houses one of the most important art collections in Europe, laid out and arranged in the most up-to-date manner. At any hour of the day in any season of the year the paintings can be seen to the best advantage in the light owing to an intricate system of mobile roofing. Special attractions are the Armoury and Maria Amalia's boudoir resplendent with small mirrors set in the tiled walls. In front of the palace and open to the public is the magnificent Capodimonte Wood, the Bois de Boulogne of Naples.

One of the rooms in Capodimonte Palace.

Masaccio, The Crucifixion.

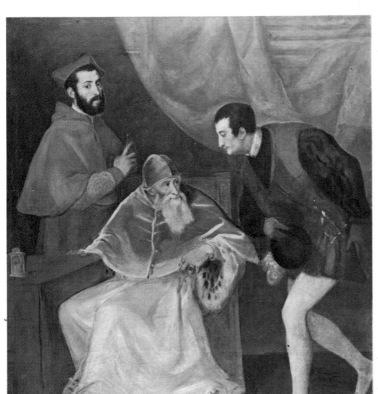

Titian, Pope Paul III with his Nephews.

21

Colantonio, St. Jerome and the Lion.

Titian, Danae.

Botticelli, Madonna with the Child and Angels.

Giovanni Bellini, The Transfiguration.

Brueghel, The Parable of the Blind Men.

Panorama of Naples seen from the **Certosa** (Charterhouse) and **San Martino Museum.** Without wishing to offend, the museum can be said to be remarkable for its picturesque staginess. Ships from Bourbon times and spectacular cribs are all mixed up with objects of interest from 18th and 19th century Neapolitan history. At times it seems like a museum of " pop " art where you get an odd feeling of aesthetic pleasure merely by coming into contact with the things themselves. If you look out over the gulf from the balcony you will not forget either the sinusoidal outline of Naples or the sound that arises from the huge city, like the echo you hear in a shell when you put it to your ear.

Eros punished by Venus.

National Museum (Museo Nazionale) - Frescoes in a museum which no one wishing to appreciate the achievements of Greco-Roman art and civilisation can afford to miss. The works reproduced here are only a tiny part of the treasures on display in the museum which is rightly considered to be the most important of its kind in the world.

Venus and Mars.

Marine life.

Paquius Proculus and his wife.

Chalice with parrots and doves.

The Battle of Alexandria.

Three other aspects of Naples: the business side seen as you look down from the **Corso Vittorio Emanuele.** Upper right, an aerial view of **Palazzo Donn'Anna,** a building which seems only half finished and has its foundations in the sea. It had the reputation of being under a curse for having been inhabited by dissolute ladies of royal blood, but actually they were not so bad as they were painted. Lower right, one of the beaches on the coast at **Posillipo** called La Gajola. Close by is the fishing village of **Marechiaro** with many good restaurants. It has been immortalised in the famous song by Salvatore di Giacomo to whose memory you will find there a commemorative tablet.

POZZUOLI   SORRENTO

Below, the **Temple of Serapides** at **Pozzuoli.** Upper right, view of **Sorrento.** Lower right, one of the figures of the tarantella as danced in Sorrento. Pozzuoli to the north of Naples and Sorrento to the south are two picturesque seaside towns, seaside also in the sense that the sea is the only source of their economic life. They are ancient towns, famous in Roman times.

Pozzuoli is supposed to have been the scene of the amusing adventures related in the "Satyricon" in the time of Nero, and is an important and well equipped international port for fishing vessels. Sorrento is a high-class holiday resort, prim and select, while Pozzuoli is gay and attractive with the bustling life of workaday people. On some days the scene in the harbour with all the fishing boats at anchor seems as if taken from an old print.

ISCHIA

Left, a view of Ischia Ponte; below, **Capri, I Faraglioni** (the Rocks); right, **Capri, Marina Grande**, and below, **Marina Piccola** with the stretch of water of the " Canzone del Mare " and the profile of Saracena Beach. Ischia and Capri are the two islands in the Gulf of Naples and are a sort of annexe to the city. There is a saying that all men can be divided into three groups: those who have seen Ischia and Capri, those who intend to see them, and those who are coming back to see them again.

CAPRI

The Emperor Augustus was very much attached to Capri, and Tiberius actually made it the capital of the Roman Empire. Since then it is almost impossible to count the number of illustrious people who have made it their abode. Even Lenin honoured it with a brief visit. Ischia is less inaccessible and a place for family holidays. Its waters are a cure for arthritis. Like those of Capri, its wines are the quintessence of sunshine rather than the juice of grape.

IL VESUVIO

A view of **Vesuvius** that does not belie the reality. Austere and all yellow with broom, it is here shown in all its mighty solitude just as the poet Leopardi described it, existing as if quite apart from the rest of the world, but yet an integral part of the artistic landscape of Naples and Pompeii. Its famous volcano is responsible for the preservation of an ancient city intact just as it was when it was buried under the ashes. Neapolitans go in fear of it but would be sorry to lose it. They can tell at once what the weather will be like by looking at its summit to see whether it is clear or cloud covered. To see one fine morning the pine-shaped column of smoke arising from it is a sign of good omen for all.

POMPEII

by CARLO GIORDANO

About the 8th century B.C. a group of neolithic families belonging to the Osci began to take up their dwelling at a point not far from the coast of the Tyrrhenian Sea. They built a village on a small hill of prehistoric lava by the mouth of the River Sarno, then navigable, and on the slope of Mt. Vesuvius, an inactive volcano. After a time Greek mariners came to establish a tradng post near their village and created a civilised community into which the natives were absorbed. They called the place Pompeii from the Greek word *pompeioi* meaning traders or merchants. In the course of time Pompeii grew and became the port for all the towns in the hinterland. In the struggle between Etruscans and Greeks for the control of the seas, it fell first to one side and then to the other. From 600 to 530 B.C. it was under the sovereignty the Greeks of Cumai who built there the Doric temple to Hercules and introduced the worship of Apollo. Then the Etruscans took over until 474 B.C. and built the temple to Apollo and probably made the first attempt at a town plan. When the Greeks came back they made a new town plan and built a new wall of defence.

This period came to an end with the invasion of Italic tribes called Samnites who occupied the town and all the surrounding country, to which the gave the name of Campania. The invaders learned the Oscan alphabet and developed Greek civilisation to such a point that Pompeii was hardly inferior to Rome. During the three and a half centuries of Samnite rule the town was laid out as it is found today, transformed from a village occupying about twenty-two acres on the site of the present forum into a large town more than six times the size. The wall was built in successive stages with eight gates giving entrance to the main streets running at right angles (two *decumani* and a *cardo*) which, however, were unpaved.

The house of a well-to-do inhabitant in Samnite times had an entrance passage leading into a hall or atrium with the four parts of the roof sloping down inwardly so as to form a square aperture in the centre (*compluvium*) to let in light and rain which collected in a basin beneath (*impluvium*), and thence flowed into a cistern to provide water for household needs. Around the atrium were the bedrooms (*cubicula*), reception rooms (*ceci*) and storerooms (*apothechae* and *alae*). After the atrium came the *tablinum*, the master of the house's study and a gathering place for the family, and from it a passageway led into a garden surrounded by a peristyle or columned portico on to which looked the dining room (*triclinium*) and household offices. The upper rooms, of only one floor, were used as servants' quarters or storerooms. The walls were decorated in the first style with coloured plaster and divided into squares painted in relief to look like slabs of marble. The floors were also decorated with mosaics in a pattern of black and white. The houses of the Faun and of Sallustius are typical ones of the time.

The Samnites devoted no less care to the embellishment of their public buildings. To them is due the enclosure of the triangular forum by a portico of Doric columns on to which opened the Palaestra, the great Theatre with its imposing fourfold portico, and a little way off the Temple of Zeus Meilichios. The square of the civil forum was surrounded about 150 B.C. by a portico of greyish tufa stone with a double order of Doric and Ionic columns, while the fourth side was occupied by the Temple of Jove. To harmonise with the new buildings the Temple of Apollo was partially reconstructed, and facing it the Basilica, also on two levels like the forum. The first public baths, the Thermae Stabianae, were built to satisfy the taste for luxury and cleanliness of a population now completely Hellenised.

The time came when Pompeii lost her independence and became part of the expanding Roman Empire. This happened with the outbreak of the Social War in which Pompeii joined the confederation against Rome in the demand for equal rights as Roman citizens. In the spring of 89 B.C. the Roman legions laid siege to the town which was stubbornly defended. It was not till nine years later that it opened its gates to the victorious Romans and became a Roman colony with the official title of *Colonia Veneria Cornelia Pompeii* and with Latin as the official language. The coming of the Romans did not bring any great changes in house architecture. There was the addition of two other styles of wall decoration: one in plain-painted imitation of marble slabs with architectural designs and scenes from Greek mythology, as in the " Villa of the Mysteries " or the house of Obellius Firmus and of the Cryptoportico, and the other with small squares set in architectural views with a minuteness of design as to appear miniature work, as in the house of Lucretius Fronto and of Caecilius Jucundus. In the last years of Pompeii's existence a fourth style was introduced, a kind of rococo, with highly ornamental wall design like that in the house of the Vettii and of Pinarius Cerialis. Multi-coloured mosaics with wavy-line patterns and inlay work of pieces of costly marble made their appearance on the floors.

Roman magnificence was shown in the public works and buildings. Most of the streets were paved with stone from Vesuvius and the water supply was revolutionised by tying up the city with the Augustan aqueduct of Serino. In the civil forum the old portico was replaced by a new one of travertine stone from Caserta and the square completely paved; it acquired a new nobility and grandeur and was reserved for use only on solemn occasions. The *Curia* and the *Comitium*, where the annual elections were held, were likewise covered over with marble, and new temples were built to Venus, Isis, Concordia Augusta and the Public Lares, the tutelary gods of the community, while the temples of Jove and Apollo were once more done up. The old Stabian Baths were brought up to date and new ones constructed, those in the forum and the central baths. A roofed theatre for musical performances was built beside the open-air one, and on a lawn at the end of the Via dell'Abbondanza arose the great Palaestra and the Amphitheatre, a jewel of Pompeian architecture.

With its 15,000 inhabitants the town was going about its usual busy life when on the 5th February in the year 62 or 63 A. D. a violent earthquake, a warning sign of the awakening of Vesuvius, shook it to its foundations and almost entirely destroyed it. The citizens set about repairing the damage with a good will, but then shortly after midday on the 24th August 79 a black cloud in the shape of a tall pine arose from the summit of the mountain and the city was plunged into the darkness of night under a hail of lapilli and ashes with streams of seething water. On the third day the sun shone out over a ruined city buried under a layer of lava six or seven yards deep. The actual number of victims will never be known; those found during the excavations amount to two thousand.

No attempt was made after the catastrophe to repopulate the town and for all intents and purposes it disappeared from the map. Subsequent volcanic eruptions, the spread of malaria in the district, and especially the continual raids of Saracen pirates along the coast during the Middle Ages made the place a wilderness and a danger spot shunned by man. An architect, Domenico Fontana, while working on a hydraulic scheme between 1594 and 1600, cut through the fields on the site of the amphitheatre without the least awareness of the nature of the archeological finds. It was not until 1748 that under Charles III official excavations were undertaken after the position of Pompeii had been indicated from some inscriptions. When Italy became a united country the work took a scientific turn and eventually led to the discovery of three fifths of the city as we see it today.

PORTA MARINA - Pompeii is entered from the west side by what is now called Porta Marina. The road that descended steeply downwards from it was once the shortest way from the city to the port. We do not know what its ancient name was, perhaps the same as used today, perhaps *Porta Portuensis*, or more likely *Porta Neptunia* from a temple to Neptune by the sea. The gate was remodelled after the war with Hannibal as is shown by Samnite additions made in 150 B.C. and others were made by the Romans who used their characteristic *opus reticulatum* of concrete faced with regular pieces of stone. It had two passageways covered by a barrel vault, the narrow one for pedestrians and the other for mules, the rise being too steep to allow for vehicles, and there was a double wooden gate raised a little above ground level so that the water could run underneath when it rained.

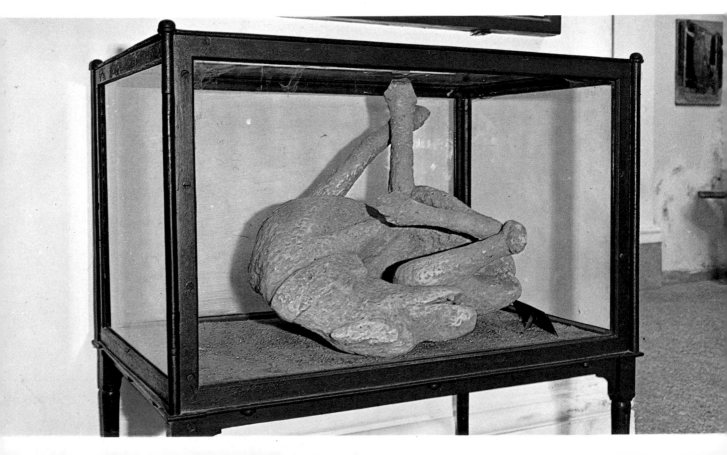

ANTIQUARIUM

Cast of a young woman lying face downwards with her head resting on her right arm and her body stripped of her garment except for her shoulders on which a good part of the shape of the dress is still preserved. She was among the last of those overwhelmed by the catastrophe.

Statue of Ephebus - This statue of Ephebus, a copy of models of 5th century B.C. Attic sculpture, was found in the house of *Marcus Fabius Rufus* who came from Rome with other settlers and must have been a relation of the dictator *Quintus Fabius Maximus* (" the Delayer ") as be bore the same family name. As is known from the discovery of the Lychnophors Ephebus in the house of *Publius Cornelius Agetes* (Reg. I, Ins. 7, no. 10), this statue was used for the practical purposes of a fruit-stand, a custom which may seem odd to us but was not uncommon at the time in the homes of the wealthy, as recorded by Lucretius in his *De Rerum Natura*.

Cast of the watchdog in the house of Orpheus (Reg. VI Ins. 14 no. 20). - Forgotten by his master *Vesonius Primus* in the general panic he was left tied up at the entrance to the house. As long as the length of his chain allowed, the dog kept climbing up on the layer of ashes but when he could no longer do so he died suffocated while vainly attempting to get free.

Cast of a mule-driver crouching down by a wall of the Great Palaestra in a vain attempt to escape by shielding himself with his cloak against the whirling ashes about to suffocate him. The mule was also found not far away.

The technique of making these casts was first discovered by Fiorelli, by pouring liquid plaster into the cavities left in the hardened ash by the bodies of the dead.

THE BASILICAS - They were situated for the most part near the Forum and served as courthouses, then as places for business dealings, and finally as centres for recreation and gossip, so that the term *subbasilicanus* for an idler or lounger passed into common speech. **The Basilica,** already in use from 78 B.C., is the largest public building in Pompeii; its main entrance is in the Forum with a four-doored hallway and two statues on the sides. Twenty-eight Ionic columns on a brick flooring divide it into three naves decorated in the first style. At the end of the building is a platform reached by wooden steps which served as a tribunal for the judges, faced by rows of columns and underneath a cell, probably for persons awaiting trial.

TEMPLE OF APOLLO - Built at the height of the Samnite age, about the 3rd century B.C., the temple has a portico supported by 48 columns which took the form of Corinthian ones in the restorations in the age of Nero, stuccoed at the base to prevent the edges from being worn away. Along the walls were painted scenes from the Iliad which was very popular in Pompeii, such as the wrath of Achilles, the death of Hector and the ransom of his body. Statues added to the splendour of the sacred edifice: on the right Hermophroditus, Mercury and Apollo shooting with the bow, on the left Venus and Diana, the latter also as an archer. A stairway of 17 steps with the altar of sacrifice in front and a pillar holding a sundial to the left of it led up to the inner part which was surrounded by 30 Corinthian columns with six in the foreground.

West portico of the Forum - The Romans began transforming the old Samnite forum and bringing it up to date by replacing the weak tufa stone with limestone from Caserta, which also from a distance gave the same effect as marble. They respected the original height and arrangement, the Doric order of the ground plan, and the Ionic order in the upper gallery from which the spectators watched fights between gladiators which were held in the Forum before the Amphitheatre was built. Unfortunately the work was still unfinished by the time of the great earthquake and the final destruction of the city. Under the portico was to be found the *mensa ponderaria* for controlling the measures used by the merchants dealing in the Forum. It consisted of two tables of tufa stone in which eight cavities were cut out to correspond to the official measures of liquids and grains. The original is now in the National Museum in Naples and the copy that has been put in its place is not a very good one.

View of the Forum from the south-east end. The sight of the Forum with its imposing ruins never fails to impress the beholder. In the foreground can be seen the Samnite portico of brownish tufa stone along which were situated the other municipal buildings, the **Curia**, and the **Comitium** at the corner where the annual elections were held. Passing along **Via dell'Abbondanza**, the most important street in Pompeii, you arrive at the east portico with the building that **Eumachia** constructed at her own expense for use as a wool market, for which she received the honorary title of public priestess from the grateful citizens. This is followed by the Temple of Vespasian with the marble altar adorned with scenes of sacrifice in the centre, the Temple of the Public Lares (guardian gods of the city), and the Macellum (the food market). At the far end the Temple of Jove stands up above, and in the background Vesuvius still looks down threateningly from its fateful summit.

TEMPLE OF JOVE - The Temple of Jove, or *Capitolium*, flanked by two triumphal arches (one was later removed), occupies the whole of the north side of the Forum. Excavated in 1817, the temple was built by the Samnites in the second century B.C., and then enlarged by the Romans and dedicated to the worship of the three deities Juno, Minerva and Jove, a huge bust of whom was also found and is now in the Naples Nation-al Museum. The vestibule was laid out with 12 Corinthian columns, six on the front and three each side, while the interior with the images of the gods had eight Ionic columns on either side surmounted by an equal number of Corinthian ones and a flooring of mingled mosaic and marble. In the basement a small door on the east side leads off to rooms which were probably used as the public treasury.

North-east corner of the Forum and Arch of Tiberius - In this stretch of the Forum, which still preserves a good deal of the Roman paving, there was another entrance into the square adorned with a marble triumphal arch with the statues of Nero and Drusus in the niches. A fragmentary inscription points to its having been erected by Tiberius. To rid the Forum of the shops that had been installed there and keep it reserved for the civil and religious authorities, the old Samnite building called the **Macellum** used as a covered-in market was remade in the Imperial age for the sale of foodstuffs under the supervision of food inspectors.

Via degli Augustali. The Augustals were the priests in charge of the worship of the emperor Augustus and gave their name to this street which serves as a model of a Roman city thoroughfare. According to the Roman historian Livy, they should be paved with hard flintstone, and for this purpose Pompeii used lava rock, from Vesuvius, a material that could easily be found in large supplies, but they also inserted blocks of stone at intervals as convenient crossings from one sidewalk to the other, especially after water collected in the roadway when it rained. The last stretch of the street near to the Forum was raised a step higher than the rest to prevent the passing of vehicles, which were not allowed into the Forum.

TEMPLE OF FORTUNA AUGUSTA - The Temple of *Fortuna Augusta*, brought to light in 1823-24, was erected at his own expense on a site he donated by *Marcus Tullius*, duumvir, augur and military tribune, as can be read in the dedication on the pediment in the interior part. A better place for a temple to Augustus could hordly have been found in the whole of Pompeii. It stands high on a hill and is reached by a flight of steps ending on a platform with the altar in the centre and enclosed against trespassers by a railing. Four Corinthian columns on the front and three on the sides supported the pediment and the roof of the vesibule. The inner hall contained the statue of Fortuna Augusta, while others were set in four niches, in one of which was that of Augustus himself, hailed as *parens patriae*, the Father of his Country. Pompeii showed its gratitude to the donor of this splendid building, a copy on a smaller scale of the Temple of Jove in the Forum, by erecting a monumental tomb to him at public expense outside the Stabian Gate.

FORUM BATHS - Calidarium - The Forum Baths, uncovered about 1823, have their entrance from Via della Fortuna through a passageway leading to the changing-room (*apodyterium*) with a seat made of masonry and wooden lockers against the wall for leaving clothes in. In front is the cold room (*frigidarium*) with a circular marble bath and an opening in the roof to let in light and sun. To the right you enter the *tepidarium*, a room tepidly warmed by a large bronze brazier. Then follows the *calidarium*, the sweating room, which was heated by a nearby furnace through a system of double walls and furnished with a marble washing basin, the gift of the duumvirs Aprus and Rufus.

VIA DI MERCURIO - the Street of Mercury. While the Street of Abundance with its numerous shops was the Main Street of Pompeii and the business centre (at some points it was more than fourteen yards wide), the Street of Mercury, likewise forbidden to vehicle traffic, ran right through the fashionable quarter. It starts with a triumphal arch, on which an equestrian statue seems to be that of the emperor Caligula, and ends at the city wall in front of a defensive tower which has now been reconstructed. Along it are to be found a number of interesting houses, those of the **Large Fountain** and the **Small Fountain, of Castor and Pollux, of Adonis, of Meleager,** and **of Apollo,** as well as a public fountain, engraved on the pilaster of which is a grotesque mask of Mercury, the god from whom both the street and the fountain take their name.

HOUSE OF THE LARGE FOUNTAIN. Nympheaum - (Reg. VI, Ins. 8, no. 24).
After the conquest of Egypt the Romans brought from the East this type of
fountain in the form of a niche and generally decorated by brightly-coloured
polychrome mosaics with figures of masks, birds and arabesques in imitation of
designs of oriental carpets. In this house, as in others in Pompeii, there is no
peristyle but, instead, a colonnaded front garden in the middle of which is a
fountain of this kind. From a bronze mouth in the centre of the niche, under
the head of a river god, the water flowed out in a slender stream on to a flight
of six steps adorned on the sides by two grotesque masks of marble, and at the
bottom a small bronze statue of a boy holding a dolphin on his shoulder.

HOUSE OF CASTOR AND POLLUX. (Reg. VI, Ins. 9, no. 6-7). **Atrium.** This house shows us one of the few examples of a Corinthian atrium with the roof supported by more than four columns. — in this case there were twelve — giving it a grace and charm enhanced by an artistic fountain spurting water into the impluvium basin. At the bottom of the garden can be seen the shrine of the Lares, the household gods who were honoured with wreaths on festal days and at full moon, and invoked on all solemn family occasions. The newly-wed bride offered them a coin when she stepped over the threshold for the first time; the youth on entering upon manhood hung his boy's garment round their neck before putting on the *toga virilis*, the manly gown; when a member of the family returned from war or from imprisonment, his weapons or his chains were laid beside them.

View of Pompeii from the Tower of Mercury - Behind Pompeii, illuminated by the sun after an age-long silence, stretches the plain watered by the river Sarno, according to Pliny the happiest countryside imaginable, where nature rejoiced to show her power and her beauty together, and where the mild breeze from the idly-flowing river refreshes the air at night. On the horizon the Lattari mountains, home of flocks of sheep rich in milk and wool, slope gently down to the shore at Sorrento with the gleaming coast of Capri beyond.

Oven and mill in the Via Consolare (Reg. VI, Ins. 3, no. 3). To overcome the economic crisis that followed on the Social Wars many middle-class families went into business and installed shops, laundries or bakeries in their houses. In this house the west side was kept for residence while the garden was turned into a bakery with four grinding mills operated by donkeys, an oven, a storeroom, a stable, and a salesroom. The lower part of the mill consisted of a cone of stone (*meta*) resting on a fixed base, and on this a hollow double cone (*catillus*) was rotated either by hand (*mola manualis*) or by an ass (*mola catillus*). The grain streaming down into the funnel of the *catillus* was crushed between the two faces of the grindstone and issued in the form of flour into a round lead container at the bottom of the mill. According to the type of flour three kinds of bread were made: dark brown (*rusticus*), medium white (*secondarius*) and white (*candidus*).

HOUSE OF THE FAUN (Reg. VI, Ins. 12, no. 2). The House of the Faun, unearthed 1830-31, is the finest example of a wealthy pre-Roman dwelling because of its size (it occupied a whole block), the nobility of decoration in the first style, and the profusion of mosaics covering all the floors. Built in the second century B.C., it has taken its name from the statue of the dancing faun in the impluvium, and first belonged to the local family of the Satri and then to the Cassii, of Roman extraction, who settled in Pompeii after it became a colony. One of the family, Cassius Saturninus, was famous in Pompeii as a lawyer and a teacher of law (*iuris doctor*) with a large following of pupils. Through two hallways, one four-columned in the Greek style, the other in the Tuscan order of the Italic style, the latter with the salutation HAVE (Hail!) on the entrance and with two shrines to the household gods in the vestibule, you enter the house itself which, like that of Trimalcius, had four dining rooms, one for each season of the year.

HOUSE OF THE VETTII - (Reg. VI, Ins. 15, no. 1).

Peristyle - discovered in 1894-95, this house, the most admired of the ancient world, belonged to two rich merchants, the brothers Aulus and Restitus Vettius and for this reason affords us the best example of the rather exaggerated taste of the newly-rich middle class in the period of Nero. For the first time in the history of the excavations it was decided to leave everything here just as it was found so that the visitor could see for himself just what a Pompeian house looked like. Through the vestibule with the figure of a Priapus as a protection against the evil eye you enter the atrium with fine paintings of boys on the black wainscot and the remains of two chests. Leading off are a number of rooms: three bedrooms and reception rooms wonderfully decorated in the fourth style. From here you pass to the peristyle, still so fresh and alive as to make you imagine the imminent arrival of the masters of the house. The reconstruction is scientifically exact as regards the decorations of trees and flowers reproduced partly on the walls and partly through the holes left by the roots in the ground. The pleasure of the greenness and sunlight was enhanced by the charm of the water which still flows through the original pipes and gushes out from the numerous statuettes into finely-wrought basins, showing us that the Romans considered the sound and sight of water an element of beauty in the house.

HOUSE OF THE VETTII - Peristyle - Detail. - In the wealthier houses the central area of the peristyle, besides being laid out as a garden, was also adorned with small statues, half-busts, small columns and animals grazing, so as to become a repository of works in marble. The peristyle of this house is decorated in this way, and when Pompeii received a water supply from the aqueduct, the statues in the gardens were transformed into pretty fountains, the sound of whose gushing streamlets, as in the villa of Pliny the Younger, mingled together in a cheerful murmur. To add to the decoration there is also a table of the type with the feet fashioned into shapes of animals, on which the household silverware was often put on show. Let us give ourselves the pleasure of walking all around the garden and admiring the two small rooms in the fourth style, one with paintings of Pentheus being torn to pieces by bacchantes, Dirces tied to the bull, and the boy Hercules strangling the serpents, the other with Ixion tied to the wheel, Pasiphaes and the bull of Crete, and Bacchus and Ariadne.

HOUSE OF THE VETTII Triclinium

HOUSE OF THE VETTII **Triclinium** - The wall decoration in the house of the Vettii becomes even more splendid in the dining-room which the owners evidently considered the most important room in the house, as they placed it so as to have the finest view on to the garden, and adorned the enrance wih more delicately-made statues as are the bronze cupids with eyes of silver. The three wooden couches on which the diners reclined have disappeared but the paintings have remained, and since the owners of the house made their money from trade they painted the black border running round the walls with scenes of men's labour and fruitful activities. It is all set in an ideal world — graceful Cupids and delicate Psyches take the place of ordinary common workmen. Starting from the right we can see Cupids at target pratice, Cupids as florists, Cupids celebrating the festival of flowers, Cupids at the grape harvest, Cupids in Bacchic procession, Cupids as winesellers. Delightful the panels underneath with Psyches and mythological scenes of Agamemnon sacrificing the hind to Artemides on the right, and Apollo with the serpent Python, and Orestes, Pilas and Iphigenia on the left. There is a wonderful picture of a bacchante with Satyrus on the end wall, and in the side panels pairs of famous lovers like Dionysius and Ariadne, Apollo and Daphne, floating in the air.

HOUSE OF THE GOLDEN CUPIDS (Reg. VI, Ins. 16, no. 7) **Peristyle** -
The site is chiefly remarkable for the scenic effects produced by the array of small
marble statues and the magnificent portico adorned with theatrical masks and
hanging marble discs (*oscilla*). Unearthed in 1903, the house belonged to *Cn.
Poppaeus Habitus* of the noble family of the Poppaei which included amongst
its members *Poppaea Sabina*, Nero's second wife. Note that the level of the west
portico is higher than that of the others, probably because it served as a stage
for a family theatre. Of the rooms giving on to the peristyle an interesting one
is the triclinium with paintings in the third style of Thetis in Vulcan's workshop,
Jason and Pelias, and Achilles with Patroclus and Brisedas, and a bedroom decorated as if with modern wallpaper and with four medaglions showing a figure
of Cupid scratched on gold leaf.

**HOUSE OF THE GOLDEN CUPIDS -
Venus Fishing** - This painting, together
with one of Leda and the Swan and of
Diana and Atheon, is in the small room
(**oecus**) to the right of the dining-room.
The portrayal of Venus in Pompeii is unlike
that found in classical art. On outdoor
paintings, especially shop signs, she is
shown with regal dignity and hieratically
robed, while in the houses of the wealthy
we see her in affected attitudes, showing off
her female charms. The model is Hellen-
istic, but the round face, curly hair, and
the numerous jewelled ornaments point to
a local type of beauty. This is the case of
this picture of her, as are those of Venus
chastising Love, Venus and Helen, Venus
and Endymion, and Venus and Mars.

HOUSE OF THE VENUS (Reg. I, Ins. 3, no. 3) **Painting of Venus in a shell.** In the age of Augustus and
after, the taste in garden painting (*topiaria*) developed
along scenic lines, depicting flowery gardens peopled
with birds, exotic ones as well, and decorated with
flowing marble fountains in an ideal and naturalistic
manner, a style that appeared again in 18th century
Italian painting. In this example a mythological theme
is introduced, Venus sailing in a shell towards the
shores of Pompeii, driven by a favourable wind which
fills the small square sail, while two cupids act as
escort. And since she is above all the peacemaker,
even the god of war cannot resist her. Accordingly
Mars is shown on the right of the goddess in full
armour but with a very unwarlike expression.

HOUSE OF LOREIUS TIBURTINUS (Reg. II, Ins. 2, no. 5) - **Garden.** We find ourselves in a garden unique of its kind in Pompeii because of its *euripus*, an artistic canal with two arms. The one from east to west was fed by a spring of water gushing from a nymphaeum adorned with wall paintings of Narcisus at the pool and of Pyramus and Thisbe. The other arm ran the length of the garden at a lower level, and at the point of intersection there was a small four-columned temple with a marble grotesque mask of the Ocean god for the water to flow through, while another temple with a statue of Hermophroditus stood in the middle of the canal. A row of statues, many of them fashioned in the Egyptian style, tall shady arbours over the canals, and a magnificent park of forest trees combined to form such an enchanting sight that the house could justly be taken as an example to illustrate the saying current in Pompeii that it is better to imitate than to envy (*imitari decet, non invidere*). This house, with its magnificent doorway rebuilt, was occupied by a Roman family from Tivoli, the head of which was *M. Loreius Tiburtinus*, a priest of the Egyptian goddess Isis. The huge garden could serve to reproduce the landscape of the Nile needed for the festival rites in her honour, and the forty amphorae still fixed in the ground probably held water brought from the Nile. Interesting rooms are the large one with scenes from the Iliad and the Heracleid, and a smaller one with a white background in the 4th style with a painting of a priest of Isis in his sacred vestments.

HOUSE OF LOREIUS TIBURTINUS · Biclinium · The spring that fed the water to the canals in the *euripus*, with a rather showy decorative scheme in the taste of the Flavian age portraying nature, was situated in this part of the garden. A place for dining stood on the water, shaded by an arbour of green and with two brick couches covered with soft mattresses on which *Loreius Tiburtinus's* guests reclined while eating from a wooden table which also stood in the midst of the green-tinted pool. The paintings of Narcisus at the pool, in which there is obviously an error of perspective as regards the face reflected in the water, and of Pyramus and Thisbe, the Romeo and Juliet of antiquity, who killed themselves for love, though they are of little artistic value are yet of great historical interest as they bear the autograph of the painter — *Lucius pinxit* — the only artist in Pompeii whose name is known to us.

THE GREAT PALAESTRA - Like all Roman colonies, Pompeii too had its *campus*, a sports ground where the youth of the city could practise all kinds of manly and warlike exercises. As the old Samnite palaestra in the triangular forum had become too small, a new and larger one was built under Augustus. It had a portico of a hundred and eighteen columns and a swimming pool in the middle (*natatio*), quite in the style of its modern counterpart, with toilets and dressing rooms and a first-aid post in charge of a doctor, *Pierus Celadus*, and a small temple with two columns in front for the guardian deity of the institute. The young athletes could find cool shelter from the sun under the shade of a double row of plane trees, and their appreciation of the joy of life is evident from one of the many wall inscriptions which reads *Iuvenes hic sumus felices* — Here we are happy while we are young.

AMPHITHEATRE - The amphitheatre of Pompeii was built between 80 and 70 B.C. by the duumvirs Quintius Valga and Marcus Portius and was meant for gladiator and wild beast shows. It can boast of being the most ancient building of the kind that we have a record of — Rome itself had to wait till the time of Augustus to have one like it — and it also has the honour of being the first building unearthed in Pompeii, for with it began the official excavations in 1748. Entrance into the arena and the first two tiers of seats (*cavea ima* and *cavea media*) was through two monumental gateways, the north one with two niches containing statues of Cuspius tand his son who were responsible for restoring the building after the earthquake. The third tier (*summa cavea*) was reserved for women and children and was entered by outer stairways up the walls along the top of which rings of Vesuvian stone were fixed to attach an awning to on very hot days.

THE VILLA OF THE MYSTERIES

THE VILLA OF THE MYSTERIES - It was excavated from 1909 to 1930 and is the most important suburban building in Pompeii for its size — it has 55 rooms on the ground floor — and for its paintings dealing with the " mystery " religion from which it has taken its name. It was first constructed as far back as 150 B.C. and subsequent enlargements brought it to its present appearance, which shows us a type of Roman villa conceived as a shrine dedicated to earthly beauty — an imperial villa in every sense of the word, as for a time it belonged to the family of the emperor Augustus, of whose wife Livia it contained a statue. Later it came into possession of the Istancidi family, natives of Pompeii and perhaps of Jewish origin, who under the procurator Zosimus were transforming it into a farmhouse and had set up a wine-press in one of the main rooms.

Passing along the hanging terrace and through a semicircular *exedra* (open-air room) you enter a black-walled *tablinum* (study) with imitation Egyptian designs in the third style, then the Tuscan atrium with a caricature of the last owner on one of the walls with the inscription *Rufus est.* On the left-hand side of the atrium there is a fine room with two alcoves in the second style. From here you pass into the peristyle with its twenty Tuscan columns (the wine-press has been reconstructed), then through the kitchen quarters you reach a rustic yard on to which opens a toilet, a bedroom with a wall cupboard, and a dining-room with festoons and vine-branches hanging betwween the columns, and finally you arrive

at the famous **Hall of the Mysteries** about which
so much has been written.

The twenty-nine figures of gods and humans painted on the walls are shown as performers in a
sacred drama whose real meaning we can only
guess at. The mistress of the house evidently
wished her reception room and bedroom to be
painted with scenes describing the rites of the
religion she followed, and has thereby left us
with the most important pictorial record of
antiquity. According to Macchioro the series re-
presents a *hierogamia,* a sacred wedding connected
with the Orphic mysteries. It begins from the
entrance door in this order: the vesting of the
woman who is to be initiated with the help of
two Eroses and a servant maid, the Catechesis
in which the mystic bride, longing to be united
to the god of the mystery, listens to the reading

by a boy priest of the precepts she must obey,
the sacred *agape* or communion with the god by
means of the holy *kukeon,* a food made of flour
and salt, the Revelation in which the fear-strick-
en bride sees in a mirror in the shape of a
chalice the god's Passion which she must relive.
Presiding at the rite are Bacchus and his mother
Kore in a central position on the middle wall.
There follows the Passion, with the purification
of the neophyte expressed allegorically by her
being scourged, and finally the Apotheosis, in
which the mystic bride, completely naked because she is now pure, expresses her joy in a
dance. The matron seated in a chair is the mistress of the house who is present at the ceremony.
The figure of Silenus dancing in the next room
gives a beautiful ending.

INDEX